Breath

Also by Thérèse Corfiatis and published by Ginninderra Press

Seasons of the Soul (with Anne Landers)
Emissaries of Light
Northern Lights
The Edge of Tranquillity
The Boy Who Loved the Moon
Handfuls of Promise
Moonlight Wine (Pocket Poets)
A Thousand Birds Were Singing (Picaro Poets)
House of Dreams
Absence of Clouds

Thérèse Corfiatis
Breath
& other poems

For Maureen and Teena, with love

Breath & other poems
ISBN 978 1 76041 912 7
Copyright © text Thérèse Corfiatis 2020
Cover photo: Thérèse Corfiatis

First published 2020 by
GINNINDERRA PRESS
PO Box 3461 Port Adelaide 5015 Australia
www.ginninderrapress.com.au

Contents

Acacia Avenues	7
Apple Pie Autumn Sunsets	8
Pigeons in Flight	9
Autumn Sunset Walk	10
Late Summer Twilight	11
A Grandson Visits	12
A Visit to Paris in July	14
Daughters and Mothers	17
Eyes	18
Lady of Letters and Feathers	19
The Guest	20
The Gardener	22
Stray Cat	23
Sacred Cows	24
A Feline Farewell	25
Laundry Rituals	27
Christine and Every Shade of Blue	28
Reunion at Hobart: Island Sisters	31
Prayer of the Child	33
What the Child Told Me	35
Temples of Blood	36
Mother and Child	38
A Woman Hurt	40
All Day She Sat	41
News Report from Christmas Island	42
Donkeys of Gaza	43
News Report from Diwanyia	46
Ward B, Room 1	48
Ancestry	49
Thoughts on a Mother's Birthday	50

On the Ferry to an Ailing Mother	51
The Five Garments	52
My Mother Died in Spring	53
A Shift of Cries	55
Bowl Haiku	56
Breath	57
Each Green Summer Leaf	58
Out Into Moonlight	59
Rain Song	60
Roses and Raven's Wings	61
Translucence	62
Sea of Dreams	63
Sleep Would Not Come	64
The Four Seasons of Writing	65
Genghis Khan	66
Portrait of a Manic Depressive	67
As a Moth's Wing	68
Rural Christmas Portrait	70
Winter Seaside Ramble	71
Midwinter Night Drive	72

Acacia Avenues

Avenues of wattle
cluster at the road's edge
a heaviness of bent colour
an arcing over of gold

It seems as if banners
of green and yellow
have swept down beside me
heralding my way

Apple Pie Autumn Sunsets

Sunsets glossy
an apple's waxen cheek,
layered clouds are piled upon each other
a pie's risen crust,
atmospheric vapours drift
scents of salty ocean
windswept sand, damp air.

Pigeons in Flight

a conglomeration of beating hearts
shifting heads, bright eyes
patterns rolled out upon the air
beaks shearing all directions
as if an unseen hand
scattered seeds of living joy
into the sky

white underbellies flash
so too the undersides of wings
flight like unfurling banners
hammered light
striking sunlit feathers
a bevy of glints and gleaming
burning heaven's blue

Autumn Sunset Walk

Road tapers off
like a long arrowhead
its tip consumed by fire

Above, clouds erupt
rosy blushes
infuse sky with colour

Wind lifts up leaves
a curling wave
of russet-ruby rustlings

Late Summer Twilight

Trees, sea-bent, appear as one –
limbs, trunks, leaves
a mishmash of variegated green
releasing breath to windswept shores.

And so, the eye is drawn heavenwards
to realms fantastic
lilac-rose, shimmering pinks and peach
trembling above a silvering sea.

In rolls and rills, shoreline unfolds
stitching tight the seam of land and sea
craggy rocks and boulders form their art
and meld into the darkening light.

A heart is stilled by peace like this
a mind released from frenzied thought
an existence knowing only now, a soul
flies free, is heaven-caught.

A Grandson Visits

For Alexander Tomas Paul, 18 weeks old

My grandson stays overnight with me,
first time without his mother –
as early morning dawns
I reflect on him,
his restless sleep and tummy aches
all gone now as he wakes
bright-eyed and grinning
knowing me, this little one
his head shifting towards my voice
eyes holding mine.

The day is ours,
fire stoked up against late winter chill,
I ferry him in pram to kitchen
or to fetch more wood outdoors –
he stares at trees and birds, happy and curious
and later, music playing on the ABC
I prepare a bottle, dancing to Strauss –
he smiles and tries to speak
little mouth contorting
into every 'oh' and 'ah' and 'wah'
his warm breath emitting tiny clouds
in the chilly room.

Much later, in the quiet evening
I nurse him, crooning softly
his face like a porcelain doll,
eyes closed, dark-lashed against soft cheeks
his little body wrapped and warm.
I could stay like this forever
awed by the miracle of his existence,
of all that came before him
and of the many things, as yet unborn, he will become.

A Visit to Paris in July

Hot, weary from walking
Maria found a place to rest
time to sit and savour,
the city closing in around her
like a dream wrapped about her shoulders.
On the pavement, café tables cluster
a couple nearby sipping drinks
conversation struck, of all things, about tea.

Words flow like liquid.

Curiosity aroused
questions asked –
I'm from Adelaide, she said
but born and raised in Hobart.

Ah, replies the gentleman.
MONA. I want to see MONA.
The famous Museum of Old and New Art.

She smiles.
This man in Paris, home of the Louvre
wants to see Tasmania's MONA.

I'm from Budapest, he says.
Oh, she answers in surprise
my father was from Budapest.

She sat in thoughts of a father who'd lived in France
fleeing Hungary at the end of World War II.
Could she have walked his very footsteps of 60 years ago?
Later, homeward bound
a certain déja vu –
Parisian streets almost familiar.

French etiquette bestows enduring memories –
strangers carry her shopping bags,
Metro seats relinquished for her comfort,
courtesy for a woman who limps.

Her artist's eye appreciates the city –
a pigeon's iridescent feathers caught in light,
textures and colour of stone,
boulangerie windows heaped high with glazed bread,
lime-green trees flanking wide, elegant boulevards
Maria's skin flecked gold and olive
as she walks beneath their shade.

She notes angles, curves and shadows
in relation to buildings
symmetry of doorways –
public gardens flushed bright with summer blooms,
majestic crouching lions –
intricate wrought iron gateways
curled and fronded vegetal motifs,
fountains tinkling water into cool marble basins.

She walks, pondering people
their connections to each other –
how the simple act of sitting in a café
drinking coffee, chatting with strangers
(are we ever really strangers?)
can reveal intimate snippets of a person's life –
a memory of her father and a man in a Parisian café
both Hungarian, both from Budapest
borders irrelevant
the language of a smile ever responsive to the human state.

Ah. Paris. A visit for her son's wedding –
conjuring up echoes of bygone journeys,
the joy of meeting French family for the first time.

She studies the way light filters through her fingers
the palm of her hand, its etches and grooves
a measure of all the lives gone before her.
She feels gratitude, thankfulness and joy
for her visit to Paris in July.

Daughters and Mothers

For Maryam

She sat alone
in the hospital ward
holding her dead mother's hand
asking forgiveness
for things said in haste
mindful of a life
that had ministered love and care to many

She stared intently
consigning each feature to memory
then stood slowly
pushing away the chair
resigned to her loss
intrinsically aware of the future grief
to assail her daughters –
to feel their burning tears and aching eyes
the weight of sorrow

It fell about her like cascading rain
each drop of water
a transfiguration
birthing rivers, oceans, shorelines –
of countless places upon the planet
where life and death occur,
a transition as natural
as a water-worn pebble
resting on a distant shore

Eyes

Eyes possess power

It is them I remember
reflecting spaces
of the world we inhabit
caught up in their swirling colours

Eyes blue-green as sky and sea
eyes shot through with amber brown
like autumn leaves –
eyes black as a crow's wing

Into them I swim deep oceans
of each and every emotion
an affinity with life's shining light –
a thing understood but unspoken.

Eyes possess power –
be it love's glance or death's dance
a newborn baby's precious cry
an adoring mother's sigh

It is them I remember –
their strength and kindness
cruelty and pain
fragility, fear, passion and shame

Lady of Letters and Feathers

In memory of Rose Stephens, 19.3.1948–28.2.2014
Mentor and friend

her letter reached me
on a perfect winter day
majestic sea and sky, clear ethereal light

she sent me feathers
folded in the page
some for my hair, some for my pillow

to give me wings at night

she sent them to remind me
of the universe's infinite precision
its wisdom and abundance

and of how this anchors each and every hope

cathedrals soared within my heart

The Guest

For Margie

As we age, our faces appear more alike,
same slant of eyes
high cheekbones, pointed chins
voices echoing each other –
strangely comforting.

Both grandmothers, mothers, wives
aunts, daughters, sisters –
we are the beginning and end of five siblings
their decades held between us.

Living far apart
time together is a rare delight,
I am my sister's dinner guest –
a quaint restaurant
once a working man's cottage in Battery Point
now upmarket, trendy.

Ivy constructs patterns
on courtyard walls outside,
green veins and capillaries
transform red brick into living art.

We are warm inside –
conversation and intimacies shared,
a candle flickers at our table
raspy voice of Edith Piaf
accompanies good food and wine.

Contentment enfolds us
as gentle hours unwind
and later as we leave
a bright full moon sails high
lighting up our smiles
moments like this a blessing.

The Gardener

I think of her
of one to whom lifelong allegiance
has been strong –
of love and care, its twists and turns
from birth to middle age
of how our journey, so entwined
(no matter our physical distance)
always found a place of tenderness, respect
and now, a black gulf of bitterness
of separateness.

I think of her, the gardener
a woman, who for decades, reveres the earth
all living things
and how for me she sowed her poisoned seeds
how, gradually, through seconds, minutes, hours
days and weeks and months
I slowly starved –
an emptiness, an ache
where once a harvest
bloomed within my heart.

Stray Cat

She came to me bedraggled
a streak through autumn leaves
across the lawn –
hunger drove her to my door.

Over time she grew to trust me
eating from a bowl
set beneath the trees,
and then, the magic moment
as I sat reading, unaware
her body arcing up
tawny eyes, pointed face
pressed against my knees,
and softly made her presence
known to me.

Sacred Cows

Heads down, cattle walk
ponderous, searching out
the next patch of green grass
large gentle eyes, hopeful
appetites appeased
with each carefully munched
mouthful.

Calves sidle close to mothers
as a winter day
fades in degrees of muted pinks
distant hills, smoky lavender
back of beasts burnished in glowing light
moving onwards
heads lowering to eat.

All that they do
is for us
giving flesh, milk and hide
so we may eat and live and thrive
honour them with space and air
and when such time comes for them
a merciful passing.

A Feline Farewell

I spent the morning trimming plants
sweeping leaves and grass
the two cats watching, inquisitive
a paw here, a paw there
a-tumbling-in-the-pile-of-cuttings
chasing each other around the garden
ambushing me with glee
(both knowing it was happening!)
a leap, an acrobatic twist
a-two-and-a-half-pike-backwards-somersault
great elegance and speed.

I laughed –
they grinned the way cats do,
Tiddle's green eyes twinkling
Bronson's amber eyes glowing

intelligent, drinking from the outside tap
quenching thirsty mouths.

And then, a gradual settling down
a leisurely cleaning of paws, faces
legs and tummy,
until they curled in a circle
napping as only cats know how.

I watched them for a long time
downhearted, their owner coming later
to fetch them to a new home,
my garden catless
birds returning to eat breadcrumbs
without the fear of looking over wingtips
wondering where the four-footed
stalking fur machines have gone
missing, no doubt, the chance to fly low
chirping mischievously, taunting
stealing biscuits from their food bowls.

We shall all miss the cats
for many varied reasons,
the sparrows will regard me
with shiny black eyes,
heads tilted to one side
and I will regard them with kindness
pleased for their good fortune.

Missing the cats in the garden
will be a group exercise.

Laundry Rituals

Basket set down
fingers weave through space and air
hands perform a dance of the ordinary
pegs grasped, clothes lifted
pleasant scent, fresh clean laundry –
above me, sky
below me, earth
body moving in between

a ritual, self-repeating
fingers reach down
hands stretch up
pegs carefully placed
garments hung in alignment
washing line adorned
with fluttering sails
on the body of a flagship called 'home'.

Christine and Every Shade of Blue

For Christine Zolnierczak Wilden, a victim of breast cancer, ten years on, 2016

Forgive me,
for writing down these memories –
I can't ask permission now.

I remember staring out the hospital window
realising none of us
can choose what we are given.

The bathroom door ajar
nurses fussed with towels
and I caught a glimpse of you
naked, weak –
head bowed like a contemplative
struggling to remain upright
a body that had birthed two daughters
skeletal now, emaciated beyond belief.

Ah, take that memory from me.

I wept quiet tears
and in my helpless state your voice jolted
'Stop that. No crying here.'

I held your hands too tight
this simple act of caring
a catalyst for pain.

We smiled for each other,
your eyes astounding
their blueness and strength catapulting
into my heart,
your faith still strong.

We shared the gift of time
and in those hours
spoke of many things.
Now I wonder
if you heard the words I said
as you drifted in and out of drugged sleep.

I leant in on your warmth
kissed your forehead, whispering 'goodbye'
and slipped out
striding swiftly down the ward
putting distance between us
knowing never to look upon your face again.

Outside the cold, bright day dazzled
my throat crushed and aching
head like an empty shell –
an ambulance sped in, siren blaring.

Each step led me away from your waning life
but as I walked
blue skies mirrored your eyes
your final lesson taught –
family, home and love
these three matter.

I live each day
in reverence of every shade of blue
holding close most faithful tender memories of you.

Reunion at Hobart: Island Sisters

(Primrose Sands)
For Lin Monash

We stood spellbound
gazing at blue-green meadows of the sea.
Across the bay, primrose sands
divided land from water –
violet hills hung vaporous on the air.

Fading sunlight caught her from behind,
she stood against a burnished backdrop of endless sky
anointed in its gentle flame.

Far in the distance
a tiny island floated on the sea
an afterthought, like a dab of paint
shaken from an unseen artist's brush and laid aside.

Our happy talk and laughter dissolved the years,
evening settling into deepest turquoise calm
we ate our supper by a sable sea
all tossed and silver-tipped in spears
tide turning with the passage of a lifting moon.

Above us glittered glorious dominions
stars cascading showers of light across the bay
heavens pulsing out their heartbeat –
the wonder of this place
acknowledged in each other's eyes.

Too soon a time to leave
great gums standing sentinel
beside the winding roads,
we drove through sleepy hamlets
to cross the River Derwent, deep and wide
Hobart town deserted under a midnight sky.

The mountain rose majestic
great buttresses of blue-black stone,
final gateway to southern icy realms,
our childhood haunt of lilac autumn mists
rolling summer foothills
howling winter winds and stark-white snow.

We did not speak,
no words were needed
as we headed towards home,
for we are sister-spirits, island-linked
its icons fused into our very souls.

The island's magic journeys with us
and tomorrow, when we part
it is this that shall sustain our hearts.

Prayer of the Child

Sometimes she could not bear
to dwell on sadness any more,
those very thoughts drove her within,
a quasi-death
repression of all feelings –
to exist in endless dread
a wretched thing.

Where was the lady she prayed to
in her veil of flowing blue?
In a world that held no comfort,
who else could she turn to?

A child subservient, controlled
unspoken worries held inside,
tears she wept were hidden
for if heard out loud
she would be punished for her cries.

Even now she remembers
how the light slipped through her fingers
as she tried to understand
the despair of upturned hands.
Were those her little hands?

A child alone,
such aching emptiness within.
No one in this world.

She carries this reality
as an imagined doll of childhood
held to her breast,
a shield, a phantom
an illusion from her youth,
of a helpless silent little creature
so very dear to her.

The doll she loved the best.

What the Child Told Me

A child plays under a grotto of trees
a dandelion held up to the sky
its filaments arabesque through air
sun-charged, spiralling high

He watches their course
neck arched back, looking up
as staring down, from the trees
peer the eyes of the dead

Transparent images
vapour-like veils
shadowy features
benign and pale

The child, pure of heart
has seen them before
unlike adults
who choose to ignore

Quiet rustlings and stirrings
strange sounds from the leaves
they simply believe
it's the wind in the trees

Temples of Blood

My heart is open for all to see.

Once it lay
curled like a tendril on a vine,
my mother's heart beating life into mine
consecrated in her temples of blood
until I was thrust out
installed into my earthly place
owner of a human face.

And so,
my heart sang and swum
in tabernacles of blood's being,
governed by cycles of growth and flowering
awaiting the future of my unborn sons
as surely as night follows day.

How fiercely I loved the flesh
that fleshed in me,
exquisite incantations and dreams
breathed hope into their unborn forms.

Beneath the thin veneer of my abdomen
I felt them shift and stir,
incredulous at the stamp
of tiny hands and feet
stencilled from within, upon my outer skin.

We are here, we are alive, they said –
and thus they came in all their rapture.

Sometimes I give little thought
to the beat of my own heart –
in moments of joy or sadness
wild fluttering reminds me of its presence
of where I come
and to where I go.

It beats on, in my sons
a part of everything they do
both them and I caught up in stardust
revolutions of planets
matter whirling through the cosmos
outward rushes of mighty solar flares –
immense designs and patterns of existence.

Together forever, never dying
always returning –
creations of love, laughter
rage, wonder
despair and awakenings.

I want them to know the depth of my love
to be unafraid,
to know humility and elation
to absorb the vibration that resonates
in the sound of the names I gave them,
so they can grow to know themselves
and thus remember me.

My heart is open for them to see.

Mother and Child

For all carers of children with disability

Our children, from the day of their birth
come to us
with all their glories and imperfections,
yet, for many mothers
there can never be a 'perfect day' –
a child struggling towards light
where each tiny step
is akin to running a marathon.

These mothers inhabit a shrinking world
growing smaller, day by day
until, like a far-off star
they become the orbit
for their ever-needy child
a life contained, beaten down by exhaustion
by sleepless, worried nights
and countless tears.

And so, the dance of madness begins –
of enduring those and their ignorance
of children spurned, devalued
mothers rejected, dejected
often hurt, alone, abandoned, impoverished
who re-invent the world each day
who teach, cherish, comfort and care
beyond all human endurance.

Such majesty and selflessness
such unrelenting courage
sets a crown upon her head
her child, its jewel held high
for all to see,
a simple wish for communion
inclusion, opportunity
for equity within, without –
a reasonable hope
for any mother to hold.

Is this not, in a country
rich and free, like ours
a birthright
a just and fair reward
for each mother
caring for her child with disability?

A Woman Hurt

a woman hurt
amongst her own
is a woman
so alone

a heart grieves
for all her pain
it seems a life
played out in vain

her love, her toil
cares and needs
unrecognised
a soul that bleeds

what value, life
she asks of me
are some so cruel
they cannot see?

a woman hurt
amongst her own
is a woman
so alone

All Day She Sat

All day she sat and watched the restless sea
her field of vision blurring
unsettled by a sky in constant motion
earth, cloud and sea forever whirling

Silence is a wounding thing
it states an obvious truth –
he turns and looks at her with stranger's eyes
no words, no caring smile

Deep down inside her is a place
an empty grieving aching space
it held her there, hour after hour
staring out at sky and sea and cloud

All she could think about was love
how it transformed her from the first
fulfilled, consumed her every breath
it was all she ever asked

Then suddenly, a memory
of how he trembled on their wedding day
the smell of whiskey when he kissed her
she understood it now

It was not love, was not desire
its illusion wove a spell on her
he was afraid of all she needed
and now it is her need she fears

News Report from Christmas Island

2013

Were towering waves
silvered and tossed with light
reminiscent of hills encircling Kabul
or more akin to the cold, craggy peaks
of mountainous Afghanistan?

In the middle of the Indian Ocean
far from home
a boat capsized,
people floundering in water
one tiny Hazara boy
flung from his mother's arms.

A newspaper report
shows a small white coffin
carried onto a waiting plane,
inside, a soul with no name
his life extinguished like a guttering flame
this child's final breath exhaled
in freedom's name.

Who stands, who speaks
who mourns the countless years
snatched fast from him?

Sleep well, my fellow citizens
and in your dreams
I wonder if your ears
can hear his piteous final screams.

Donkeys of Gaza

For millennia these sturdy creatures
bent their backs to loads and human cargo
travelling dusty roads and byways,
hardworking, gentle-eyed, stoic by nature
they still live and work with the people of Gaza.

Animals know nothing of a destiny
and as such, the donkeys of Gaza
are subject to their owner's whim –
the dilapidated Gaza zoo
once painted them to look like zebras,
and in 2014, Hamas strapped explosives
(downtrodden people rarely possess sophisticated weaponry)
to a donkey's body and attacked Israeli soldiers.

As long ago as 1962
David Ben-Gurion* said of Palestinians
'We view them like donkeys.
They don't care. They accept it with love.'

A protector of Holocaust survivors
this leader had not understood
that to steal a people's land
is to steal a people's future, and thus
a whirling wind of chaos and war was birthed
each newborn baby's cry in Gaza
a lament to displacement and exile
a cry for justice and retribution.

Amidst this confusion and misery
the donkeys of Gaza plod ever onwards
carrying huge loads on building sites
often exhausted and overworked,
replacing cars
(there is no fuel to run them)
and cleaning rubbish from the streets –
some have even been photographed
swimming with Palestinian boys in the sea near Gaza city.

One spring day, two millennia ago
a donkey with a proud gait
and shining eyes
carried a man named Jesus
over a carpet of palm branches into Jerusalem –
he, a king amongst men
shared a message of peace and love
still with us today.

This Jewish man founded, unbeknown to him
a Christian empire –
how could he have ever foreseen
what humanity would do in his name?

Somewhere in Gaza
another little donkey breathes and walks
and dreams at night, as all donkeys do
of one sweet and glorious day
when a man with gentle hands
leads them towards an earthly paradise.

Peace be upon him. Upon him, peace.

---

* David Ben-Gurion was the primary national founder of the state of Israel and the first prime minister of Israel, 3 November 1955–26 June 1963

News Report from Diwanyia

South of Baghdad

Tall and gaunt
the father stands helpless
mournful dark eyes stare at the camera.

His tiny daughter, premature
came too early
into a broken city.

Doctors are exhausted –
nothing works
no electricity, equipment, medicine –
just sheer human will.

The mother lays deathly ill
a hard birth
not knowing her little one has died.

The pitiful scene unfolds before me.

I watch this man
wrap his tiny daughter in a towel
place her body reverently
into a cardboard box.

He walks away with her, alone.

For Iraqi babies
there is no tomorrow
too much pain, too much sorrow.

What has happened to us
as we sip our tea
desensitised to such misery?

Ward B, Room 1

His voice leapt on the telephone.

'My daughter,' he announced loudly
for those to hear and know he's not alone.

After years of silence
both near to breaking
we find ourselves somehow clinging on.

The heart lifts out of its sluggishness
kind words vibrate upon the tongue –
a fragile healing struggles
for without such thoughts and deeds
what goodness can there come?

'Hello, Dad.
How are you today?'

Compassion compels me
to banish bitterness
to the dark place it belongs.

Ancestry

My maternal convict ancestor
endured Norfolk Island's miseries,
hundreds of lashes for impertinence
long periods of isolation
for thieving tea, sugar, tobacco.

Somehow he survived
was granted a ticket of leave,
settled and married in Hobart town.

The light of freedom revealed
new hope beyond prison walls,
his resolve born out of a dark place of horror.

Each step of his life began and ended on an island.
Shall it be so for me?

Thoughts on a Mother's Birthday

Today she looks ill and worn
a face drawn and tired,
on this, her 80th year
no amount of happiness can hide.

Our love and longing
is rolled tight, like a ball
waiting to be thrown
unsure of the distance.

Hours slipped away
like vapours and mist
into a past
I can no longer retrieve.

On the Ferry to an Ailing Mother

Crossing Bass Strait to Devonport

Fields of canola
slip by the window,
thoughts of my mother
lost in ribbons of road.

My sister had rung me
mum worsening, ailing
a journey cut short
a desperate need to get home.

Too many thoughts
crush in on my soul,
a beautiful weight
like fields covered with gold.

Sailing home to you, Mother
at night, by the sea
ocean holds me and rocks me
as once, you did me.

I pray in the starlight
silver waves churned with foam
journeying back to the island
to you, to our home.

The Five Garments

For Beverley and her five children

my mother moves in ways caught up in pain
her tender core enmeshed within its tangled skein
her life unravelling, fraying at the end
a swathe of glorious cloth needing gentleness to mend

come all of you who love her, with your smiles and your song
weave deft allegiance to her fabric, make it strong
help repair the damaged threads worn by toil and hurt and age
so these, her final moments are a just reward of days

a time of knowing richness in a life well spent
her five children, living garments
spun from labour, love and hope
to enfold and hold, protect her, in an all-embracing cloak

My Mother Died in Spring

Beverley Amelia Ravanelli, born 7/8/1937, died 6/10/2017

My mother died in spring
when bluebells thrust up great walls of flowers
stocks drifting sweetest scent upon the air,
days lengthening into longer, azure dreams
of all her childhood spun, one glorious moment
as she took her final breath.

My mother died in spring
when magnolias burst in fists of colour beyond compare,
deep-pink camellias, large as saucers
nestling in against the glossy greens,
trees wreathed in living jewels
a world she loved, of bright and joyful tones
like the roses she painted, to hang upon her wall.

My mother died in spring
when blackbirds chorused by her windows
in the darkness, long before dawn
and other birds replied, in twittering, joyful calls
sweetest notes fell upon her ears, far sweeter
than any other sung before
from leafy kingdoms, a world enthralled.

My mother died in spring
it seemed this time, a season arraigned in beauty
unsurpassed as any gone before,
death waiting by her door
as hot tears fell, all selfish though
whispering our goodbyes
because we had to let her go.

My mother died is spring
as oceans glistened coppery-silver in burnished light,
I kissed her eyes and cheeks
and held her hands, and asked she float away
into the light,
to drift upon calm seas
whilst above her, planets swept around the sun
to know her circle is complete, how she'll live on
in my first grandchild, soon to come.

A Shift of Cries

Some people say that stones cry out –
I have always thought
graveyards to be silent places.

My thought shifts –
perception lifts and sharpens
or is it the sudden movement of trees
sporadic flashes of sunlight
through branches, limbs and leaves
bringing focus to my brain?

Trees raise themselves up
lifting bold outlines against the sky –
it is the 'living' state connecting me to them,
those silent spaces speaking within us.

I notice fresh buds unfurling
on blossoming trees –
I had not noticed them before.
Perhaps they noticed me.

The tiny moment elevates,
everything becomes magnified
beautiful beyond description.

Unlike the stones my bones cry out.

When I am gone, let silent places sing.

Bowl Haiku

spring rains form a pond
blackbird wings shake off water
a bowl of sweetness

Breath

Long before dawn's light lifts up the sky
I am wide awake –
husband sleeps, warmth radiating
against my curving spine.

I lay quietly
pondering
how many days
invested in his every breath
how many for our sons?

Decades fall behind me
countless moments like a million falling leaves –
all gone
except for now, this very one.

I swear
this day I'll hold so dear
knowing those ahead
shall be far less
than the ones I've left behind.

I close my eyes
hear my breath draw in, draw out
and ask for one more time.

Each Green Summer Leaf

Separation
from those I love
creates deep sadness in my heart –
yet a residue of joy remains.

Sometimes their very existence
seems a strange abstraction
as if their flesh had never been
their lives as fleeting as clouds
drifting across a sky, only to disappear.

In my contemplations
each green summer leaf
already turns its face inwards
towards autumn
the warm day becomes chill
overlaid with melancholy.

At night
beneath the beautiful immensity of stars
I imagine them watching me
from high and haunting heavens.

Do not chide me, my departed ones
for in all my yearning
you still journey with me
our bond strong, unbroken.

Out Into Moonlight

Out into moonlight
honeyed notes of birds
fill up silences
heaven's stars abloom
like wreathed flowers
a million petals set afire

the little town sleeps
sea purring out its soothing rhythms

a red camellia
falls to earth
its muffled thud
distracts the eye
its movement enough
to break the spell

Rain Song

Rain falls hard
wash away, wash away, wash away
all troubles washed away

Rain falls hard
a comfort true, a cleansing
wash away, wash away, wash away

Rains falls hard
a steady beating drum
wash away, wash away, wash away

All troubles washed away

Roses and Raven's Wings

In dreams
they come to me,
my mother, resurrected
younger, radiant
speaking words again –
my long-dead father, smiling
black hair glossy as a raven's wing

I woke amazed
it seemed so real and fresh
but then, a pall of sadness
because they'd left each other decades ago
a lonely, sad affair for him
for her, a second chance at life

and then
another memory lifts up –
a vast lake
my mother reclining in a boat
trying to catch roses with her fingertips
as they float by

steady rain falls in silken vertical veils
a million silent arrows
pierce the lake's still waters –
pin-pricks of memory, already fading
flown away on raven's wings

Translucence

Gentle rains, transparent veils
a soft illusory translucence
of liquid blossoms falling in the space about them.

Beyond those watery films
senses are heightened
fresh scent of wet eucalyptus, damp earth
waft in the music of raindrops
connecting one to the other.

Sea of Dreams

Relentless rain
drums fingers on the iron roof
night swallows the deluge
with a hungry mouth.

Rain spears across windows
giving an illusion
of a world
slipped sideways.

Lulled by rain's rhythm
my bed becomes a boat
afloat on an ocean of weariness
drifting into a sea of dreams.

Sleep Would Not Come

Sleep would not come. Rising
restless from my bed
I wandered out into the night –

my eyes drank in a heady potion made of stars.
Flat sea shone like sun-shot glass
mirror for a pumpkin moon
sailing high overhead – plump, round and ripe
flesh asking for the taking.

Mobs of gulls in feathered clouds
moved deep into a sable-stained unending sky,
their flight had placed much thought in mind
(same questions pondered as a child)
where do we come from?
where do we go?

Humanity sets me apart from
nebulae, amoeba, tree
yet such beauty cleaves into my heart
and forms the truest part of me.

I only know this moment now
no more, no less am I
I cannot answer where and how
I cannot answer why.

The Four Seasons of Writing

Winter's fields lay bare and wet
a time of quiet reflection,
fireside nights
recall maps of the inner heart
a thousand yesterdays remembered
strands of memory woven
thought flaring up like little flames

Springs's brighter days
erupt in green, blossom and scent
a catalyst for fresh growth,
all is a rush of new beginnings
a coursing creativity –
energetic spaces where
words stream like scudding cloud

Summer's golden hours
harbour troves of visual glory,
nights of warmth and intimacy
beneath a flushed-full ripeness
of trees and starry heavens,
inspiration rising up of its own accord
mind and hand alive with fire

Autumn's space is meditative
a gearing down
richness found in vibrant colours,
profound contemplation
space for a mind to fly free
for thankfulness –
to harvest the wonder of words

Genghis Khan

Legend says the grave of mighty Temujin* was trampled by 800 horses
the riders executed to prevent its discovery.

Somewhere on the endless central Asian steppes
the Lord's bones lay.

Rain and wind and time have not revealed them,
his conquests and visions forever held in history's page.

No grave marker erected, he lives and breathes
a hero to his descendants, revered in the hearts of warrior men.

---

* Genghis Khan, born Temujin, c. 1162–18 August 227, Great Khan of the Mongol Empire

Portrait of a Manic Depressive

She sings in the park
to an invisible audience
and dreams of Russian world supremacy.
She remembers, as a toddler
a camera's tripod
and how it held the power to enthral.

At six, she quoted Shakespeare
and now, as an adult
proclaims his words
to be a spiritual heartland.
The Koran is a guiding light.

Ideas and sentences flood in torrents
bearing down on any who'll listen –
her novel on religion
is a work in progress.

She skips on her toes
like a ballerina,
red painted lips startle –
her shopping sprees astonish
back seat of the taxi overflows.

Lack of sleep wears her down
mind and body succumb –
months spent in recuperation.

Her life is like a revolving door
twirling relentlessly
unable to halt its spin.

As a Moth's Wing

For Philip

His skin, pale gold
fragile as a moth's wing –
veins flutter and pulse
in sinewed sculptures of his neck.

Drugged eyes
glassy, remote
speak to either splendid
or chaotic dreams.

The long scar of his wound
rises up in stapled revolt,
a row of silver sentries –
breath reminiscent of crushed herbs.

Nurses whirl in and out like dervishes
machines blink and hum, alien symphonies
conducted by needles, tubes, drains –
orchestras of blood, water and waste.

On a bedside cabinet lilac roses huddle
soft infolded plum centres
offer up perfumed beauty
like a silent prayer.

Anxieties and pain
are measured in long days
until one morning he looks stronger
walking outside for a while.

It's as if a cloud
moves away from the sun
offering hope
showing the way home.

Rural Christmas Portrait

Strong westerlies bluster in,
paddocks, straw-yellow, leached dry.
Galahs, parrots, plovers and gulls
compete in a summer sky.
Grey-green seas fling breakers
to a sweeping windswept shore,
silver necklaces of frothy spume
like tinsel dropped on a floor.

In the distance music sounds
a Christmas parade's bright song,
the town's main street crowded
with happy faces of its young.
Santa waves from the back of a ute
reassuring them Christmas will come.

Some say Christmas is not the same
as it was in days gone by,
but there's a gleam of something special
in everybody's eye.
The message lives for all of us,
it speaks to love and peace and joy,
as we remember the timeless story
of a mother and her newborn boy.

Winter Seaside Ramble

Low and lovely light
gently caresses skin
cold air tingles
chill pressing ever in.

Lilac-mauves unfold
every shade of pearl within
symphonies of wonder played
horizons growing dim.

Light fades, not in a sudden rush
but one long breath exhaled of love
sweet mother earth enfolding all
as stars emerge, above.

Midwinter Night Drive

Burnie to Ulverstone – north-west coast, Tasmania

View Road
a steep downwards descent,
deserted streets, except for cats
sheltering under hedges or patrolling gutters –
eyes reflected in the car's headlights.

From this high vantage point
swaths of shining sea spread out like a vision
Burnie town, a scene set upon a winter stage
held in brilliant moonlight,
its port stuffed full
container ships, vessels, giant cranes
rail yard's tracks disappearing into darkness
a pair of slithering snakes –
industrial ugliness softened by moonlit shadows.

On the highway out of town
great mounds of woodchips resemble crumbling pyramids
memories of another life buried deep within their dust
a million birdsongs in a million trees
forgotten forest choruses
ghostly echoes of beating wings
of soft rainfall soaking mossy ground,
mist trailing fingers on the wind.

To the left, Bass Strait
constant companion for another 30 kilometres
to the right, a steady flow of traffic
folk returning home at day's end
eager to be in from the cold.

Sea is ever magical
a breathing living entity, and so
a conscious turn made into Sulphur Creek
a quieter coastal route,
ocean tumbling onto pale sandy beaches
rocky outcrops staring outwards like surreal sentinels
a seabed littered with old shipwrecks
a place often too wild, too savage
but on this night, tranquillity abides.

A possum dawdles across the road –
a soft 'beep beep'
sees it disappear into surrounding scrub
free to forage and roam.

Road curves around the bay –
brilliant stars distract
concentration lapses
and then, as if in warning
a flock of seabirds shriek –
the driver smiles.

Ahead lies sleepy Penguin village
its foreshore dappled silvery-blue
tall pines line the road's verge
cohorts of pearly trunks and outstretched branches.

House lights create a soft amber glow
shadowy shapes of occupants blur across glass
flesh melting into feathery shades –
chimney smoke curls upwards in long plumes.

The coastal road winds higher
as craggy cliffs dip down to sea,
Bass Strait sparkling like rumpled taffeta
fabric stretched against horizons
a line defined by moonlight
as if drawn by an otherworldly hand.

The Three Sisters* rise up
like tousled heads surfacing water,
high tide marks visible on stone –
dark velvet ribbons around three necks,
the islands, a haven for summer seabirds
empty now, touched only by wind and sea and light.

Cliff-bound to the right
road bends like an archer's bow –
while to the left sea sings
whistling arrows shot from a quiver,
railway tracks raised up on stony beds
a man-made imposition –
vaults of air flung high
the space between earth and sky
a kingdom for wedge-tailed eagles.

Goat Island juts up from the sea
a local landmark walkable in low tide,
while far off in the distance
deep lavender hills stand bold against heavens –
lights of Devonport
glimmering like bioluminescence.

Ulverstone approaches
set in its cradle
a town divided by the Leven River,
long sandy beaches on either side
like two embracing arms.

South Road is wide and welcoming –
trees bunched in groups
interspersed amongst large gardens,
a gradual slowing down,
house set back from the road
like a crouching cat –
pathway to the door
illuminated beneath a canopy of dazzling stars
blessing the traveller's return.

Midwinter journey is done.

* The Three Sisters Islands are three small, rocky islands located in Bass Strait lying 500 metres off the north-west coast of Tasmania, between Ulverstone and Penguin.

www.ingramcontent.com/pod-product-compliance
Lightning Source LLC
Chambersburg PA
CBHW062152100526
44589CB00014B/1792